PREVENTING SEXUAL HARASSMENT, A MANUAL FOR SUPERVISORS AND HR PROFESSIONALS

By Brad Wolff

All rights reserved. Without limiting the rights under copyright reserved above, no part of this publication may be reproduced, stored in or introduced into a retrieval system, or transmitted, in any form, or by any means (electronic, mechanical, photocopying, recording, or otherwise) without the prior written permission of both the copyright owner mechanical, photocopying, recording, or otherwise) without the prior written permission of the copyright owner.

THANKS TO Patrick Breen, who proofread this whole book and without his help this book would never have been published.

Table of Contents

INTRODUCTION 6
DEFINITION 8
THE POLICY 8
DISEMINATE 9
HOW TO REACT 12
OUTSIDE THE CONCERN 15
THE WORLD 18
⍰ 22

Thank you for selecting my book. I have done my best to make it one of the best decisions you make during your life. If you got any benefit from this book please leave a much-appreciated review. I realize that your time is valuable so here is a hyperlink to the page where you can leave a review would really be a big help to me because Amazon will help me sell more books. Here is the easy Hyperlink:https://www.amazon.com/dp/B077SZZW5W

INTRODUCTION

Ever since the Harvey Weinestein case and Me Too movement the topic of sexual harassment has enjoyed a resurgence. The main question is usually "how to avoid it"? That is what this book is about. The prevention of sexual harassment has gained new respect with publishing. This book is a diamond in the rough. All it needs is a little polishing to be the answer to the question. What is sexual harassment? Not only will it be defined but this book will answer all of your questions about sexual harassment. No other book tells you as much! Not a day goes by without another man or more often woman making new allegations of sexual harassment. It is difficult to know what to do in the current environment. This book addresses what a supervisor or Human Resources professional should address in the present situation.

.

This book is written for managers and HR professionals to inform you on what how to act personally or do for the concern and how to behave to avoid to avoid liability. This book is an instruction on how to avoid liability either personally or for your employer.

DEFINITION

What is sexual harassment? The best way to define it is to see what the Federal agency charged with enforcement of the law governing the subject. The U.S. Equal Opportunity Employment Commission (EEOC) defines workplace sexual harassment as unwelcome sexual advances or conduct of a sexual nature which unreasonably interferes with the performance of a person's job or creates an intimidating, hostile, or offensive work environment. Sexual harassment can range from persistent offensive sexual jokes to inappropriate touching to posting offensive material on a bulletin board. Sexual harassment at work is a serious problem and can happen to both women and men.

Mutual state and federal laws shelter employees from sexual harassment at work. Sexual harassment is a form of sex of the turn of discrimination under Title VII of the Civil Rights Act of 1964. While Title VII is the foundation level for sexual harassment claims, states have sexual harassment laws which may be even more strict. Refer to the laws of your state for accurate data.

I actually had a man we were checking since he had just become a supervisor over a predominately female workforce. He expressed dismay when instructed on the company's sexual harassment policy. He strongly complained about it because one of his main reasons for striving for a supervisory position was the pick of the women was one of the major reasons for the promotion. This is a perfect example of how we have changed as a society we almost expected a male in a supervisory position to engage in sexual harassment. As a result, most investigations are not covered by evidence. We were all conditioned not to believe any woman who came forward complaining of such conduct. The situation was often the classic he said she said. The woman was never believed. Well, that has undergone a major shift. All the woman has to do is make an allegation. Suddenly asexual harassment is at the forefront of an all our minds since the Harvey Weinstein outing. This book offers sound advice that can be followed in other countries with different laws

THE POLICY

The first step that must be undertaken by the Human Resources Department is to draft and publicize policy prohibiting sexual harassment. The policy should create a three-person committee that investigates every complaint of sexual harassment. The committee should include the HR Manager, a respectable man, and one woman. Each person has one vote and has the power to interview potential witnesses. After they agree that no more investigation is warranted they vote guilty or not guilty. The whole committee must be in agreement to conclude the investigation. The committee is given broad powers to investigate complaints and call witnesses. If the verdict is guilty the committee then discusses the action or penalty. At this point, the HR reprehensive on the committee must tell then man/woman that a statement that a sexual harassment charge has been filed against them concealing (as much as possible) who made the charge. At this point the offender is told that a charge of sexual harassment is has been lodged against them.

Sexual harassment is something that happens more often than people think. The Center for Disease Control has the most accurate figures. Based on their keeping track of such things 1 in 5 women and 1 in 71 men will be a victim of sexual assault in their lifetime. Also, according to the CDC. And every 8 minutes, that victim is a child. Meanwhile, only 6 out of every 1,000 perpetrators will end up in prison. 321,000 people are victims each year.

Under Title VII there are two recognized types of sexual harassment -- 1) quid pro quo and 2) hostile work environment.

Under the quid pro quo form of harassment, a person in authority, usually a supervisor, demands that underlings bear sexual harassment as a condition of getting or keeping a job or job benefit. A single occurrence of harassment is sufficient to sustain a quid pro quo claim (e.g., superior demands sleep with you her/him in order to keep your job), while an outline of harassment is typically required to qualify as a hostile work environment.

Hostile work environment harassment is grounds for legal action. Elements which courts analyze in determining whether a hostile environment harassment claim is valid to comprise:

    Whether the conduct was verbal, physical, or both;

    Frequency of the conduct;

    Whether the conduct was hostile or clearly aggressive;

    Whether the alleged harasser was a co-worker or supervisor;

    Whether others joined in ratifying the harassment; and

    Whether the harassment was directed at more than one individual or singled out the victim.

In any sexual harassment case, the alleged victim will have to meet a subjective and objective standard. In other words, the plaintiff must show that:

    he/she genuinely believed the conduct was hostile, abusive, or offensive; and a reasonable person in the plaintiff's position would objectively believe the conduct was hostile, abusive, or offensive.

DISEMINATE

Training for all supervisors and managers is an item that the session must be attended. Any class must be mandatory. If the site is large schedule several sessions so that it is possible for them to attend one.

Title XII only applies to employers with 15 or more employees. For companies with less than 15 employees, state law governs -- and most states have enacted laws covering such situations. If either quid pro quo or hostile work environment harassment can be established, employers may be liable for compensatory (monetary loss, pain, and suffering) and punitive damages. Liability may depend on who committed the harassment (superior or co-worker) and what action the company took to correct it. Employers are responsible for the conduct of supervisors and managers. Employers also have a responsibility to keep their employees free from harassment by non-employees (e.g., customers, vendors, suppliers, etc). Managers are liable for sexual harassment between co-workers if they knew or should have known about it and took no steps to stop it. The existence of a company grievance procedure alone does not automatically insulate employers from liability. Employers should also take action against sexual harassment once they are aware it is happening.

Actual sexual harassment policy makes clear the illegality of sexual harassment and defines a clear and appropriate complaint process while a respecting the confidentiality of the victim. Moreover, such a strategy encourages witnesses or victims to report the behavior on the day that it happens: reprisal against persons reporting harassment is illegal and will not be tolerated.

Once concluded, an organization's sexual harassment policy should be disseminated to all employees and a copy posted in an available and prominent location. It should be sent by email to every employee. Employers should also consider development seminars or workshops on sexual harassment to promote company-wide facts of the policy.

Many states have drafted state prevention model policies for employer use. Other employer finds concerning may be obtained from federal employment discrimination enforcement agencies such as the Equal Employment Opportunity Commission (EEOC) and state fair employment agencies, or national organizations fighting sexual harassment,

If the harassment is committed by a superior and:

There is palpable employment action taken to the quarry (firing, demoting, negative changes in assignments or responsibilities), the employer is liable.

The harassment is hostile work environment, then the employer is liable. The employer's defense to liability is that it 1) exercised reasonable care to prevent the harassment and took prompt corrective action to stop it once made aware, and 2) the employee unreasonably refused to take advantage of the corrective measures.

It seems counter-intuitive to put so much in a paper on sexual harassment but if you want to be given credence by outside agencies an employee must know the how to file a complaint. This is the most important part of any policy.

If the harassment is committed by a coworker:

    the employer is liable if it knew or should have known about the harassment unless the employer took immediate corrective action.

Give examples that the audience can relate to:

standing too close to the person.

Complementing on what she is wearing

Another worker is hitting on her

Tell them that their job includes two things their own personal actions and that of everyone they supervise.

Let them know that they will be told if they are ever the subject of a complaint. Now is the time to tell them that complaints are often won but the claim of sexual harassment retaliation is then found to have merit.

They will be told that they have a charge of sexual harassment against them but will not get the identity of the person who made the complaint.

Employee training is to some degree something that has to be done. The main reason for doing this is to let all employees know that they are encouraged to complain if they feel that they were the victim of sexual harassment.

The employees must be told that in such a case they will go directly to a committee formed for the sole purpose of handling complaints of sexual harassment. It has the power to actually discharge the offender. Many times, the committee is torn as to what to do because the supposed harasser threatens to sue if action is taken. Complainers would be free to sue if they were not pleased with the committee's decision. There is this internal route is put in place to handle complaints without interference from an outside agency. Employees are encouraged but not required to use the internal procedure created only to handle such complaints.

HOW TO REACT

Employers are prohibited from retaliating against employees who file complaints. While this may hold some comfort, employees know that in the real-world retaliation in some form may occur. Therefore, it would be wise to get a copy of your personnel file before you file a complaint. If you have this in hand, you'll have documentation of positive past work performance and evaluations in the event that the company retaliates by demoting or transferring you while claiming you have a poor track record. In these litigious days, the wisest move is to expect the worst (a lawsuit to settle your claim) and prepare accordingly.

First, you should personally try to end it. If that doesn't work, look at your employee handbook or manual and see what policies the company has in place and take your complaint to that level. No matter what, you should document everything (each instance of harassment, what

actions were taken by superiors, etc.), as it will only add to the asset of your case.

Personally, Inform the harasser his/her actions are offensive

While this is the most difficult act for victims of harassment, it is ultimately the most effective method of ending the behavior. The harasser may not even be aware that her/his behavior is offensive, and it is always best to "nip" it in the bud before inappropriate comments or jokes, left unrestrained, turn into something uglier.

If you are uncomfortable facing the harasser, write a short letter or email letting her/him know you want the behavior to stop. If you're uncomfortable doing this, tell a supervisor. If you write a letter, make a copy. If you write an email, send it from a company email address. You'll want to document every action that's taken by the committee, along with the response.

If there is no lessening of the harassment after personal appeals to stop, then escalate your complaint to the next level. Be sure to follow all company protocols dealing with sexual harassment (and document everything to show that you took every action the company recommended). At each step, if you don't get the proper response from management, continue escalating the complaint up the chain of command.

The reason for following company procedures and documenting everything is simple: if you don't follow company procedures and give them a chance to stop the harassment, you will likely lose in court. So, complain within the company, let them know about the situation, document it, and keep backups in files away somewhere safe away from the workplace. If he/she is fired it is proof that swift action was taken to prevent future harassment.

Documentation does not end at keeping emails and memos to co-workers and supervisors. You should write down each instance of harassment as they happen. This includes specific information, in addition to date and time, such as the people involved, onlookers if any, their reactions, how the event made you feel and affected your work and general wellbeing, etc. Keeping a journal of such events will strengthen your case and allow you to recall events clearly without worrying about forgetting or misremembering details.

Documenting the harassment is important for use as evidence in a case or complaint.

You should:

- Photograph or keep copies of any offensive material at the workplace.

- Keep a journal with detailed information on instances of sexual harassment. Note the dates, conversation, frequency of offensive encounters, etc.

- Tell other people, including personal friends and co-workers if possible.

- Obtain copies of your work records (including performance evaluations) and keep these copies at home If the person alleged to have been harassed decides to file a complaint with an outside agency, it is advisable to consult an attorney, although they are not required to retain counsel in order to file. Attorney referrals can be obtained by contacting local (e.g women's centers, rape crisis centers) or national women's organizations, their union (if member), specialized employee interest groups, law schools, legal aid community services, state Fair Employment Practice (FEP) agencies, or state Equal Employment Opportunity Commission (EEOC) offices. In addition, your friends and professional contacts may know suitable attorneys.

Interview all attorneys who may potentially represent you. At the very least, any attorney you choose must specialize or have experience in employment discrimination law. Ask the attorney if she/he has prior experience dealing with sexual harassment cases, and what the outcomes of those cases were. Pay attention to the attorney's demeanor and to your "gut" feeling about this person. Once you retain an attorney, pay attention to how she/he treats your case. Are your phone calls returned within a reasonable timeframe? Does your attorney take your concerns into consideration as she/he develops your case? Like anyone else you may hire, you have the option of firing an attorney who does not adequately represent you.

In order to file a civil lawsuit under Title VII, you will first have to send your complaint to the EEOC, the federal agency that enforces Title VII. Only after the EEOC investigates and no settlement is forthcoming can an alleged person harassed file a Title VII lawsuit. State agencies may have different policies, so be sure to investigate those further. Make sure to file a claim before any federal or state statutes of limitation expire.

A male coworker has made what sounds to you like a sexual innuendo, but you can't be sure. However, this same individual has made similarly inappropriate comments toward women in the past. Is it harassment? And if so, do you have a strong enough case to file a claim? It's not always so easy to make this determination, but an experienced attorney can help.

Employers are responsible for the conduct of supervisors and managers. Employers also have a responsibility to protect their employees from harassment by non-employees (e.g., customers, vendors, suppliers, etc). Managers are liable for sexual harassment between co-workers if they knew or should have known about it and took no steps to stop it. The existence of a company grievance procedure alone does not automatically insulate employers from liability. Employers should also take responsibility to take action against sexual harassment once they are aware it is occurring.

Sexual harassment is not mutual and is unwelcome. It is rude, demeaning behavior and is usually about the abuse of power. In fact, sexual harassment psychologically hurts the women involved and the work atmosphere. According to the National Council for Research on Women, women are 9 times more likely than men to quit their jobs, 5 times more likely to transfer, and 3 times more likely to lose jobs because of harassment (The Webb Report, June 1994). There may be serious economic consequences as a result of sexual harassment. A woman's job status may be jeopardized and he/she may lose wages if she/he is fired or takes extended leave to avoid the harasser.

The 1994 Merit Systems Protection Board Study of sexual harassment noted that women in traditionally male-dominated occupations such as construction, policing, the military are more likely to be harassed. Additionally, other studies have found that harassment is more commonly found in female-dominated workplaces where a majority of women earn low wages and the management is predominantly male (A victim of sexual harassment may file a legal claim even if she/he has tolerated the behavior for fear of retaliation or losing their job

OUTSIDE THE CONCERN

Contact a qualified employment discrimination attorney to make sure rights are protected.

According to a current issue update from the U.S. Equal Employment Opportunity Commission (EEOC), sexual harassment occurs, "when submission to or rejection of this conduct explicitly or implicitly affects an individual's employment, unreasonably interferes with an individual's work performance or creates an intimidating, hostile or offensive work environment

The U.S. Equal Opportunity Employment Commission (EEOC) defines workplace sexual harassment as unwelcome sexual advances or conduct of a sexual nature which unreasonably interferes with the performance of a person's job or creates an intimidating, hostile, or offensive work environment. Sexual harassment can range from persistent offensive sexual jokes to inappropriate touching to posting offensive material on a bulletin board. Sexual harassment at work is a serious problem and can happen to both women and men.

Both state and federal laws protect employees from sexual harassment at work. Sexual harassment is a form of sex discrimination under Title VII of the Civil Rights Act of 1964. While Title VII is the base level for sexual harassment claims, states have sexual harassment laws which may be even more strict. Check the laws of your state for more information.

This book will outline the two types of workplace sexual harassment, employer liability, and strategies and procedures to put an end to the behavior.

With the legal standards for sexual harassment at work in mind, victims of harassment also bear the burden of attempting to end it.

Sexual harassment can occur in a variety of situations. These are examples of sexual harassment, not intended to be all-inclusive.

- Unwanted jokes, gestures, offensive words on clothing, and unwelcome comments and repartee.

- Touching and any other bodily contact such as scratching or patting a coworker's back, grabbing an employee around the waist, or interfering with an employee's ability to move.

- Repeated requests for dates that are turned down or unwanted flirting.

- Transmitting or posting emails or pictures of a sexual or other harassment-related nature.

- Displaying sexually suggestive objects, pictures, or posters.

- Playing sexually suggestive music.

When an employee complains to a supervisor, another employee, or the Human Resources office, about sexual harassment, an immediate investigation of the charge should occur. Supervisors should immediately involve Human Resources staff.

Employees need to understand that they have an obligation to report sexual harassment concerns to their supervisor or the Human Resources office.

The policy handbook needs a:

- sexual harassment policy,
- general harassment policy,
- policy about how sexual harassment investigations are conducted in your company, and
- a policy that forbids an employee in a supervisory role from dating a reporting employee and that details the steps required should a relationship form.

I think the workplace is one of the logical locations for people to meet and fall in love, as long as the employees engaged in the relationship follow common sense guidelines. However, dating your reporting staff is never appropriate. After creating these policies, you need to train all employees about them.

Managers and supervisors are the front lines when it comes to managing employee performance and needs from work. First, and most importantly, you do not want a workplace culture that allows any form of harassment to occur. Out of your commitment to your employees and your company, harassment, in any form, is never to be tolerated.

As an employer, demonstrating that you took appropriate steps is crucial. In fact, demonstrating that you took immediate action and that the consequences for the perpetrator were severe, is also critical. The front-line leader is usually the person initiating and following through on those steps, so they have to feel confident about what they are doing.

Any form of harassment can create a hostile work environment including sexual harassment and how it is addressed. The court's definition of what constitutes a hostile work environment has recently expanded to coworkers who are caught up in the situation, too.

As you think about sexual harassment and other forms of harassment in your workplace, keep these facts in mind.

- The employee harassing another employee can be an individual of the same sex. Sexual harassment does not imply that the perpetrator is of the opposite sex.

- The harasser can be the employee's supervisor, manager, customer, coworker, supplier, peer, or vendor. Any individual who is connected to the employee's work environment can be accused of sexual harassment.

- The victim of sexual harassment is not just the employee who is the target of the harassment. Other employees who observe or learn about the sexual harassment can also be the victims and institute charges. Anyone who is affected by the conduct treated his or her lover differently than they were treated.

- In the organization's sexual harassment policy, advise the potential victims that, if they experience harassment, they should tell the perpetrator to stop, that the advances or other unwanted behaviors are unwelcome.

- Sexual harassment can occur even when the complainant cannot demonstrate any adverse impact on his or her employment including transfers, discharge, salary decreases, and so on.

- When an individual experiences sexual harassment, they should use the complaint system and recommended procedures as spelled out in the sexual harassment policy of their employer. The investigation should be conducted as spelled out in the policy.

- The employer has the responsibility to take each complaint of sexual harassment seriously and investigate. The investigation should follow these steps listed in the policy.

- Following the investigation of the harassment complaint, no retaliation Is permitted, regardless of the outcome of the investigation. The employer must in no way treat the employee who filed the complaint differently than other employees are treated nor change his or her prior-to-the-complaint treatment. If it is determined that the employee lied, however, disciplinary action is necessary.

- In United States labor law, a hostile work environment exists when one's behavior within a workplace creates an environment that is difficult or uncomfortable for another person to work in due to discrimination. Common complaints in sexual harassment lawsuits include fondling, suggestive remarks, sexually-suggestive photos displayed in the workplace, use of sexual language, or off-color jokes.[1] Small issues, annoyances, and isolated incidents typically are not considered to be illegal. To be unlawful, the conduct must create a work environment that would be intimidating, hostile, or offensive to a reasonable person. An employer can be held liable for failing to prevent these workplace conditions, unless it can prove that it attempted to prevent the harassment and that the employee failed to take advantage of existing harassment counter-measures or tools provided by the employer.

- A hostile work environment may also be created when management acts in a manner designed to make an employee quit in retaliation for some action. For example, if an employee reported safety violations at work, was injured, attempted to join a union, or reported regulatory violations by management, and management's response was to harass and pressure the employee to quit. Employers have tried to force employees to quit by imposing unwarranted discipline, reducing hours, cutting wages, or transferring the complaining employee to a distant work location.

- Thus, federal law does not prohibit simple teasing, offhand comments, or isolated incidents that are not extremely serious. Rather, the conduct must be so objectively offensive as to alter the conditions of the individual's employment. The conditions of employment are altered only if the harassment culminates in a tangible employment action or is sufficiently severe or universal.

THE WORLD

Women around the world are beginning to tell their stories and expose the universality of sexual harassment in their societies. A 1992 International Labor Organization survey of 23 countries revealed what women already know: that sexual harassment is a major problem for women all over the world. Sexual harassment affects women's mental and physical health as well as their social and economic status. The level of tolerance for sexual harassment varies from culture to culture. For information on the incidence of and remedies for sexual harassment in a variety of countries,

Any of the following unwanted behavior may constitute sexual harassment:

- leering
- wolf whistles
- discussion of one's partner's sexual inadequacies
- sexual innuendos
- comments about women's bodies

'accidentally' brushing sexual parts of the body

- lewd & threatening letters
- tales of sexual exploitation
- graphic descriptions of pornography
- pressure for dates
- sexually explicit gestures
- unwelcome touching and hugging

sexual sneak attacks, (e.g., grabbing breasts or buttocks)

- sabotaging women's work
- sexist jokes and cartoons
- hostile put-downs of women
- exaggerated, mocking 'courtesy'
- public humiliation
- obscene phone calls
- displaying pornography in the workplace
- insisting that workers wear revealing clothes
- inappropriate gifts (ex. lingerie)
- hooting, sucking, lip-smacking, & animal noises

- pressing or rubbing up against the victim
- sexual assault
- soliciting sexual services
- stalking
- leaning over, invading a person's space
- indecent exposure

Compiled by Martha Langelan in Back Off! How To Confront And Stop Sexual Harassment and Harassers

Sexual harassment is a form of sex discrimination when it would not have occurred but for the person's gender. It is covered under. Some of the most recognized forms of sexual harassment are:

- Direct sexual advances or propositions, including higher-ranked employees, asking for sexual favors.
- Intimidating or excluding women employees to jeopardize their employment status.
- Creating a hostile workplace for women by using sexist jokes, remarks, or pinning up sexually explicit or pornographic photos.

The law remains unclear whether a woman "who is not herself the object of sexual harassment might still have a hostile environment claim." (Women and Sexual Harassment: A Practical Guide to the Legal Protections of Title VII and the Hostile Environment Claim by Anja Angelica Chan, JD, [Harrington Park Press: New York, 1994]).

Offensive and demeaning behavior does not have to be tangibly detrimental to the job to be considered sexual harassment.

Ignoring problems of sexual harassment can cost the average company up to $6.7 million a year in low productivity, low morale, and employee turnover and absenteeism, not including litigation or other legal costs. Following clear and proactive formal policies against sexual harassment in the workplace is one way to prevent lawsuits and drops in productivity and efficiency. ("Sexual Harassment in the Fortune 500", Working Woman, Dec. 19, 1988).

Stopping Sexual Harassment

If possible, and if the harassment is not too severe or violent, directly confronting the harasser may be useful. Also, although having protested is not necessary for a claim, it would strongly strengthen a claim.

In Back Off! How To Confront and Stop Sexual Harassment and Harassers, Martha Langelan recommends taking these steps:.

- Do the unexpected: Name the behavior. Whatever he's just done, say it, and be specific.
- Hold the harasser accountable for his actions. Don't make excuses for him; don't pretend it didn't really happen. Take charge of the encounter and let people know what he did. Privacy protects harassers, but visibility undermines them.
- Make honest, direct statements. Speak of obscenities, serious, straightforward, and blunt.

- Demand that the harassment stops.

- Make it clear that all women have the right to be free from sexual harassment. Objecting to harassment is a matter of principle.

- Stick to your own agenda. Don't respond to the harasser's excuses or diversionary tactics.

- His behavior is the issue. Say what you have to say and repeat it if he persists.

- Reinforce your statements with strong, self-respecting body language: eye contact, head up, shoulders back, a strong, serious stance. Don't smile. Timid, submissive body language will undermine your message.

- Respond at the appropriate level. Use a combined verbal and physical response to physical harassment.

End the interaction on your own terms, with a strong closing statement: You heard me. Stop harassing women.

You may also file an internal complaint through the appropriate avenues offered by the organization's policy on sexual harassment if it has one.

If the victim is a union member, reporting the harassment to the union steward may garner support and secure a potential ally. According to the National Labor Relations Act, unions must represent and aid their members in stopping sexual harassment, a form of discrimination. There are strict limits on filing grievances. They must usually be filed within 6 months of the date of the incident you are complaining about. If the union is uncooperative, the victim may file a complaint (also within those 6 months) with the NLRB (National Labor Relations Board).

- Filing your claim with the EEOC (under Title VII of the 1964 Civil Rights Act).

You must file a claim with the EEOC within 180 days of the last incident of harassment to begin the process of obtaining relief under Title VII. An EEOC claim can be filed in a manner to protect the victim's identity. Title VII covers all public and private employers in the United States, as well as U.S Citizens working for a U.S. company based in a foreign country. Complaints can be filed through EEOC district offices are located across the United States. The Civil Rights Act covers only companies with 15 or more employees. State fair employment agencies (FEP) laws may be more generous and extend to smaller companies.

suggests considering the following checklist:

Sexual Harassment	Flirting
feels bad	feels good
one-sided	Reciprocal
feels unattractive	feels attractive
is degrading	is a compliment

feels powerless	in control
power-based	Equality
negative touching	positive touching
unwanted	Wanted
illegal	Legal
Invading	Open
Demeaning	Flattering
sad/angry	Happy
negative self-esteem	positive self-esteem

Originally appeared in USA Today

- to be the person harassed but could be anyone affected by the offensive conduct.
- Unlawful sexual harassment may occur without economic injury to or discharge of the victim.
- The harasser's conduct must be unwelcome.

STOPPING IT

Broadly speaking, sexual harassment is any unwelcome sexual advance, including unwelcome verbal or physical sexual conduct. Over the years, sexual harassment lawyers have developed labels for the two types of sexual harassment cases that exist. The first is referred to as "quid pro quo" sexual harassment and it occurs when an employee is required to engage in sexual conduct as a condition of employment or to gain a promotion or other employment-related benefit. Quid pro quo cases involve a "trade" of sexual services in exchange for the promotion or other benefits at work. The second type of sexual harassment, which is known as "hostile work environment" occurs when sexual words or conduct in the workplace create a hostile, offensive or intimidating work environment.

When most people think of sexual harassment in the workplace, they are probably thinking of quid pro quo harassment. Quid pro quo harassment happens when an employee is required to engage in sexual conduct–including submission to unwelcome advances–as a condition of that person's employment. In other words, quid pro quo harassment occurs when an employee must submit to sexual conduct in order to keep his/her job or receive a promotion or other benefit

Hostile work environment harassment is different from quid pro quo in that the unwelcome conduct does not need to come from a direct supervisor or someone in authority and does not need to be a condition of the victim's employment. Consequently, the standard for establishing a claim of hostile work environment harassment is somewhat higher.

Simply put, a victim can state a claim for hostile work environment harassment when verbal or physical conduct of a sexual nature in her place of employment is so extreme that it materially alters the conditions of the victim's employment. Courts look to several factors to determine whether a hostile work environment exists: 1) whether the conduct was verbal or physical or both; 2) the frequency of the conduct; 3) whether the harasser is a supervisor or simply a coworker; 4) whether the conduct is objectively offensive; and 5) whether the conduct was directed at more than one individual. No one factor is necessary or dispositive.

The Supreme Court has made clear that Title VII is not a general workplace "civility code. Incidental and occasional comments are therefore not enough to establish a claim. Although an isolated incident may be sufficient if it is truly outrageous–such as rape or assault–generally the conduct must be pervasive and frequent. The conduct must also be objectively severe, not simply subjectively offensive. At the same time, the conduct need not be so severe that it leads to a complete nervous breakdown. The Supreme Court has made it clear that an abusive work environment may detract from an employee's job performance or discourage an employee from remaining on the job even if it does not have a debilitating effect on the employee's psychological well-being.

www.ingramcontent.com/pod-product-compliance
Lightning Source LLC
Chambersburg PA
CBHW051533240526
45471CB00019B/1341